WIN WITH US OR WATCH US WIN

Turning Dreams into Dollars: A Black Woman's Guide To A Fundable Enterprise

By: Nathalie Noisette

DISCLAIMER

The contents of this workbook are provided for informational purposes only and do not constitute legal or financial advice. The information, tips, and strategies presented herein are intended to offer guidance and are not guarantees of any kind. While this workbook is designed to assist individuals in becoming more effective grant candidates, it is important to understand that following the advice given does not ensure or guarantee success in winning grants. Users of this workbook should not rely solely on the information provided for making legal, financial, or other important decisions. The authors and publishers of this workbook disclaim any liability for any direct, indirect, incidental, or consequential damages resulting from the use of the information contained within. It is always recommended to seek the advice of qualified professionals for legal or financial matters.

You're in The Right Place

What people are saying about Mental Money

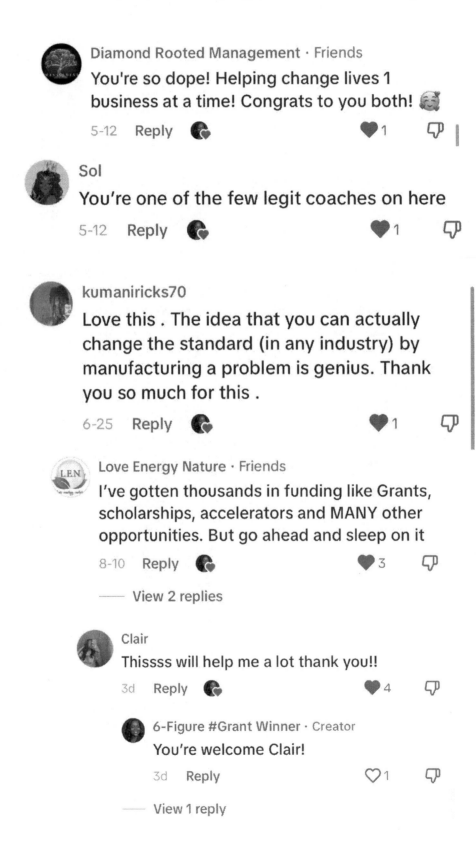

Diamond Rooted Management · Friends

You're so dope! Helping change lives 1 business at a time! Congrats to you both! 🥳

5-12   Reply   ❤ 1   👎

Sol

You're one of the few legit coaches on here

5-12   Reply   ❤ 1   👎

kumaniricks70

Love this . The idea that you can actually change the standard (in any industry) by manufacturing a problem is genius. Thank you so much for this .

6-25   Reply   ❤ 1   👎

Love Energy Nature · Friends

I've gotten thousands in funding like Grants, scholarships, accelerators and MANY other opportunities. But go ahead and sleep on it

8-10   Reply   ❤ 3   👎

──── View 2 replies

Clair
Thissss will help me a lot thank you!!

3d   Reply   ❤ 4   👎

6-Figure #Grant Winner · Creator
You're welcome Clair!

3d   Reply   ♡ 1   👎

──── View 1 reply

Table of Contents

NATHALIE NOISETTE

From the moment I embarked on my entrepreneurial journey, I was driven by a single passion - to empower and uplift businesses, especially those at the grassroot level. With a proud Haitian-American heritage, I've always felt the need to give back, to help others rise, just as my Haitian migrant parents instilled in me.

My success with securing $269K in non-dilutive funding, not counting loans or revenue, is a testament to the hard work and dedication I've poured into my endeavors. And now, my mission is to light the way for others. Through the Mental Money podcast, I've reached countless listeners, sharing insights, strategies, and stories that inspire and equip. But that's just one facet of my outreach.

Online, I've dedicated myself to breaking down the intricacies of grant applications. Through strategic walkthroughs, I teach the framework to answer questions effectively, ensuring businesses stand out and are competitive. You can find those videos on YouTube. This is complemented by the "Master Plan Monday" sessions, where I offer one-on-one strategic advice on navigating the grant space. It's all about understanding the perspective of funders and aligning your business vision with their expectations.

This workbook is my next step in this mission. It will serve as a comprehensive guide, helping businesses conceptualize how funders perceive them. What are the essential elements to consider before seeking funding? How can you craft a winning strategy? This book will answer these and more.

One of my proudest moments has been partnering with the Giving Joy Foundation to fund a grant for the Fondation Luc-Eucariste in Haiti. This grant, named after the Mental Money podcast, is a testament to our collective commitment. The organization deeply resonates with me, with its focus on empowering women through health, agriculture, and educational resources. Knowing that I've played a role in supporting an initiative that aligns with my parents' dreams for a brighter future fills me with immense pride.

What I genuinely hope you extract from this workbook is more than just knowledge; it's empowerment. I want you to feel equipped with the tools and strategies needed to navigate the complex world of funding successfully. Through the pages of this book, I aim to demystify the funding process, breaking it down into actionable steps that any business can follow. It's my desire that every reader feels a renewed sense of confidence in their entrepreneurial journey, knowing they have a guide to help them secure the resources they deserve. With the right mindset and strategies in place, I believe every business can achieve the success it envisions. Together, we will create the path to a brighter and more prosperous future for Women-led Black businesses.

When it comes to business development and growth, funding plays a pivotal role. Securing the right kind of financial support can make the difference between a fleeting business idea and a flourishing enterprise that gets funded. Each area of a business, from its foundational concept to its customer engagement strategies, can influence funding opportunities. As we dig into the following topics, we'll explore how each one intricately connects with and impacts the realm of funding:

1. **Crafting the Right Business Identity**: Your business name is often the first impression funders get. A name that's memorable and relevant can make your business more attractive to investors and grantors.

2. **Visionary Business Blueprint**: Your concept defines what your business is all about. Funders want to know the core idea and how it differentiates from others in the market.

3. **Articulating Business Value**: This highlights the unique value your business offers. Clearly defining this can make the difference in convincing funders of your business's potential profitability and societal impact.

4. **Understanding Your Market**: Understanding and defining your target audience demonstrates to funders that you know who your customers are, ensuring a better chance of business success.

5. **Forecasting Initial Investments**: A clear breakdown of your start-up costs showcases your planning and foresight, assuring funders of your financial responsibility.

6. **Strategizing Business Earnings**: Here we outline how you plan to make money. Funders want to see a sustainable and scalable model before they spend.

7. **Establishing Business Foundations**: This demonstrates your business's legal standing and organizational structure, which can influence funding decisions based on liability and management efficiency.

8. **Financial Transparency & Management**: Transparent and organized financial records indicate to funders that you are responsible, and that their funds will be used wisely.

9. **Innovative Product Roadmaps**: Showcasing a well-thought-out product development strategy can persuade funders of the potential market value and demand for your product.

10. **Innovative Service Roadmap**: Like product development, a comprehensive service development plan indicates the potential for steady revenue streams.

11. **Embracing Digital Reach**: A robust marketing plan indicates to funders that you not only have a great product or service but also a strategy to make it known to your target audience.

12. **Prioritizing Customer Satisfaction**: Ensuring a positive customer experience can lead to repeat business and growth. Funders are more likely to invest if they believe customers will have a positive interaction with your brand.

13. **Building Collaborative Alliances**: These can amplify your business reach and capabilities. Demonstrating potential or existing partnerships can reassure funders of your business's growth potential.

4. **Narrative Power in Business**: A compelling narrative about your business can emotionally engage funders, making them more invested in your success. It's not just about numbers; it's about the vision and passion behind them.

As we transition from the foundational concepts that shape business success, it's important to understand that every decision, strategy, and plan is connected to create a picture of your business story. This story becomes the driving force behind securing funding and achieving your entrepreneurial dreams. With these core principles in mind, let's delve into Chapter One, where we'll examine the details of what truly gets businesses funded. Prepare to uncover the secrets and strategies that set apart the funded from the unfunded.

Chapter 1

OBJECTIVE

Learn the foundational elements that attract funders, with a special focus on the power of a compelling business name.

ACTIVITY

For our hands-on activity, we'll strategically select a name that resonates, empowers, and positions your business for success.

Chapter One: Unraveling the Mind of a Funder

At the heart of every funding decision lies a simple truth: funders are individuals or entities looking for success stories they can be a part of. They're not just blank-check machines but astute evaluators, meticulously assessing where their money will generate the best outcomes. It's crucial for businesses to understand this perspective to effectively position themselves for funding.

- **The Human Element**: Funders are inherently drawn to individuals who radiate passion, competency, and vision. The person steering the ship can significantly influence a funder's decision. Leadership qualities, past achievements, and even personal narratives all play a role.

- **The Power of an Idea**: A well thought-out, innovative idea stands out. But it's not just about newness; it's about feasibility, scalability, and potential market impact. Funders seek ideas that fill gaps in the market, address pressing issues, or introduce transformative solutions.

- **Significance of a Name**: Believe it or not, a business name can sway perceptions. Names that resonate with the business's essence, are memorable, and having market appeal can make a difference in funding considerations.

- **Not a Rescue Mission**: It's essential to demonstrate that you're not seeking funding as a last-ditch effort to save a sinking business. Instead, funding should be portrayed as the catalyst that will propel an already promising enterprise to greater and newer heights. It's about compounding your potential, not preventing your failure.

- **Funder's Motivations**: Beyond the financial considerations, many funders are driven by the positive publicity and image boost they receive from backing successful ventures. Associating with a thriving, innovative business can be a PR goldmine. The idea of getting a tax write-offs can't be overlooked. Many funders, especially philanthropic ones, benefit from tax deductions when they support businesses, particularly if they're structured as charitable donations or have partnered with one.

Securing funding is a two-way street. While businesses gain the financial muscle to achieve their dreams, funders reap the rewards of positive PR, tax benefits, and the satisfaction of backing a winner.

What's In A Name?

The name of your business is more than just a title; it's the first brushstroke on the canvas of your business, setting the tone and making an impression. In the world of funding, where first impressions often dictate the trajectory of discussions, a compelling business name can be a game-changer. It serves as an introduction, providing a glimpse into your business's ethos, values, and objectives.

Choosing the right name goes beyond aesthetics and catchiness. It needs to resonate with your target audience, encapsulate the essence of your business, and foster trust. A poorly chosen name, especially one hinting at high-risk ventures, can be detrimental. For instance, incorporating terms that suggest volatility or uncertainty can immediately raise red flags for potential funders. They're on the lookout for stable, promising ventures, and even a hint of undue risk can divert their attention somewhere else.

Your business name is a reflection of your brand's identity and vision. In the competitive arena of funding, where every edge counts, ensuring your business name aligns with your goals and doesn't inadvertently signal high risks can significantly influence your funding prospects.

In the business world, some industries are seen as 'high-risk', and the names you choose for businesses in these sectors can make a big difference.

Consider casinos and online gaming. They're all about chance. Names with words like 'Bet' or 'Jackpot' can make them seem even riskier. This industry faces many ups and downs, rules to follow, and depends a lot on how the economy is doing.

Now, think about pharmaceuticals. It's a field where new drugs are tested and made. Using terms like 'Experimental' or 'Synthetic' in a name can raise eyebrows. Why? Because these words hint at untested drugs or treatments. The drug world is tough, with many rules and the constant challenge of making sure treatments are safe.

Every industry has its challenges, and the names we choose can either add to or ease those challenges. When picking a name, it's vital to be aware of the industry's risks and how certain words might be perceived.

Other Industries and Associated Words That Are Considered "High Risk"

CASINOS AND ONLINE GAMING

This sector is all about chance. Names with words like `Bet` or `Jackpot` can make them sound even riskier. They face lots of rules, economic ups and downs, and competition.

TELEMARKETING SALES

It's all about reaching out to potential customers. But words like `Cold-Call` or `RoboCall` might turn people off. The challenge? Keeping calls professional and avoiding being seen as spammy or intrusive.

CRYPTOCURRENCY

A new financial method. However, terms like `Unregulated` or `Speculative` can sound risky. This industry faces fluctuating dollar values, security issues, and regulatory judgement.

PHARMACEUTICALS AND DRUGS

This is where new drugs are made and tested. Names with terms like `Experimental` or `Synthetic` can be red flags. The industry has many regulations and the task of ensuring treatments are safe.

ADULT ENTERTAINMENT

A sensitive area where discretion is key. Names with words like `Explicit` or `Casual` can be too forward. The industry faces societal judgments and rapidly changing online platforms.

GUNS & AMMUNITION

This industry faces many debates about safety. Words like Automatic or High-Capacity can seem risky. It's important to choose names wisely because of strict rules and public concerns.

ACTIVITY

Identifying High-Risk Words in Your Industry

Goal: Learn which words might seem risky in your business area and avoid using them.

Steps:

- Name Your Industry: Write what kind of business you have.
  - Example: If you do tech stuff, is it software, gadgets, apps, or something else?

- Look It Up: Use the internet to see what people say about your type of business.
  - Find any problems or big talks about your business type.
  - Check words that seem to show up a lot in bad news.

- Write Down Risky Words: From what you found, list words that might look bad or make people worried.
  - Example: For digital money stuff, words like `Unregulated` or `Bouncy` might look bad.

- Think About It: Look at your list. Think about how people might feel about those words. Would they trust your business less?

- Pick words from your list to avoid in your business name. Keep this list for later.

Define Your Indsutry

Risky Words

Picking the Right Business Name: Key Considerations

Choosing a name for your business is a big deal. It's the first thing people will know about you, and it can say a lot about the business itself. Here are some things to think about when picking a name:

- **Meaning**: Does the name say something about what your business does? It should give people a good idea about what you offer.
- **Easy to say**: It should roll off the tongue. If people have to struggle to pronounce it, they might forget it.
- **It's Unique:** You don't want to get mixed up with another business, especially not a competitor. Make sure the name isn't already in use.
- **Domain & Social Media Availability**: If you're making a website, check if the name is available as a web address (domain name). It's good when they match.

Picking the Right Business Name: Key Considerations

- **Copyrights & Trademarks**: Make sure the name isn't copyrighted or trademarked by someone else. This can save you from legal problems later on.
- **Spelling**: Avoid weird spellings. If people can't spell it, they might have a hard time finding you online.

An Additional Note On Legalities

When it comes to naming your business, the creative aspect is just one side of the coin. The other, equally critical side, is ensuring the name stands on solid legal ground and possesses a unique identity in the market.

Starting with legal checks, it's important to dive into trademark databases, such as the one provided by the U.S. Patent and Trademark Office. This ensures that your chosen name hasn't been claimed within your industry, preventing potential legal disputes. Alongside trademarks, there's the matter of business registries. Every state has its own, and it's essential to verify that no other registered entity has your desired name. While business names aren't usually copyrighted, drawing too close a parallel with prominent copyrighted material can be problematic. For instance, a tech company named "Apple Innovations" might raise eyebrows given Apple Inc.'s popularity. When navigating the legal aspects of your business, consulting with a legal professional can save you a world of trouble. They can see pitfalls and guide you around them.

On the front of uniqueness, a basic online search can be enlightening. It can reveal if any businesses operate under a similar name and provide a glimpse into their operations and reputation. In our digital age, the name's availability as a domain and on major social platforms like Instagram or TikTok is important. A matching .com domain, even if you don't intend to set up a website immediately, can be an asset worth its weight in gold. Local business directories, such as Yelp or Yellow Pages, offer another avenue to check for name similarities. Sometimes, feedback from industry peers or the community can highlight names that might tread too close to established businesses.

ACTIVITY

Goal: Come up with potential names for your business that resonate with your brand, are unique, and stand on firm legal ground.

Steps:

1. **Reflect on Your Brand**: What is the essence of your business? What feelings or images do you want your business name to evoke? Write down words or phrases that come to mind.

2. **Think of Synonyms**: For each word or word you've written, list down synonyms or related terms. This increases your pool of potential names.

3. **Combine & Play**: Mix and match the words and synonyms you've listed. Try different combinations. Don't be afraid to play with the words or even invent new ones.

4. **Say It out loud**: Sometimes, names sound great on paper but don't roll off the tongue easily. Speak each potential name aloud. How does it sound? Is it catchy? Memorable?

5.**Get Feedback**: Share your 5 names with 5 people. This could be friends, family, but preferably potential customers. How do they react? Their first impressions can be invaluable.

To best understand how the name resonates with people we're going to ask these very pointed questions:
- What comes to mind when you first hear the name?
- Does the name give you a sense of what the business might offer or stand for?
- Is its relevance to the business clear?"
- If you were to hear it once, do you think you'd remember it later? (ask again before the call ends to see if they remembered the name)
- Does this name remind you of any other businesses or brands? If so, which ones and why?

6. **Reflect**: After gathering feedback, take a moment to reflect. Which name aligns best with your business's goals?

Top 5 Name Selection

	Name Ideas
01	
02	
03	
04	
05	

Name:	
What was the their initial reaction?	**Are they able to say the name properly and recall it at the end of the call?**

Were they able to clearly understand what the name meant and its relevance to your business?

Did they mention that the business reminded them of any other business?

Name:	

What was the their initial reaction?	Are they able to say the name properly and recall it at the end of the call?

Were they able to clearly understand what the name meant and its relevance to your business?

Did they mention that the business reminded them of any other business?

Name:	
What was the their initial reaction?	**Are they able to say the name properly and recall it at the end of the call?**

Were they able to clearly understand what the name meant and its relevance to your business?

Did they mention that the business reminded them of any other business?

Name:	

What was the their initial reaction?	Are they able to say the name properly and recall it at the end of the call?

Were they able to clearly understand what the name meant and its relevance to your business?
Did they mention that the business reminded them of any other business?

Name:	

What was the their initial reaction?	Are they able to say the name properly and recall it at the end of the call?

Were they able to clearly understand what the name meant and its relevance to your business?

Did they mention that the business reminded them of any other business?

Before You Commit:

Now that you've picked a name for your business, it's time to make sure it's can actually be yours. This next step is about checking that no one else has the name and making it official. This foundation is key to building your business's future and ability to be funded.

☐ **Trademark Search:**

Check if the name is already trademarked. Use national databases, such as the U.S. Patent and Trademark Office, to ensure no conflicts.

☐ **Business Registry Check:**

Verify with your state's business registry to ensure no other business has registered with the same name.

☐ **Domain Availability:**

Even if you're not immediately setting up a website, make sure the .com domain (or relevant domain for your country/industry) for your name is available.

☐ **Social Media Handles**

Check major platforms (Instagram, Twitter, Facebook, LinkedIn) to make sure your selected name or a close variation is available for use.

☐ **Local Business Directories**

Browse local directories (e.g., Yelp, Yellow Pages) to see if businesses nearby use a similar name.

☐ **Copyright Considerations**

While names typically aren't copyrighted, make sure your chosen name isn't close to copyrighted material.

☐ **Name Approval (If Required)**

Some states or countries may require approval for certain words in a business name (e.g., "Bank" or "Institute"). Ensure your name is in line with these regulations.

☐ **Legal Consultation**

Especially if you're not sure or if your business operates internationally, seek advice to make sure you've covered all legal bases.

Registration

Once you've checked all boxes, proceed with registering your business name with relevant authorities to legally claim it.

Trademark it!

If you anticipate your business growing nationally or internationally, consider trademarking your name to protect it across broader territories. Also trademarking is one of the only, if not only ways to protect your business from other organizations that like to "borrow." Funders love to know that you have this protection in place.

TRADEMARK PROTECTION TOOLKIT: RESOURCES GUIDE

🔍 Find the Right Legal Support for Free:
Our carefully curated list includes reputable law clinics who offer pro bono (free) legal services. Whether you're just starting out or looking to expand, you'll find valuable resources tailored to your needs.

📓 Easy Access, Organized for Convenience:
We've organized the list to make it easy for you to find the right legal support. With clear categories and up-to-date contact information, you're just a click away from connecting with professionals who can guide you through the trademark process.

NOTES

NOTES

NOTES

Chapter 2

Discover why you started, your core values, and what is keeping you going.

For our hands-on activity, we'll uncover the "WHY" of your business.

Discovering your "why" is one of the most important steps in your business journey. Your "why" isn't just a reason; it's the heartbeat of your business. It's what gets you up in the morning, fuels late-night brainstorming sessions, and keeps you pushing forward even when times get tough. More than a motivation, it's the core purpose that drives every decision you make.

But why is it so crucial? Your "why" connects you to your customers on a deeper, more emotional level. When people understand and resonate with your reason for being in business, they're more likely to support you. It's the difference between someone simply buying a product and someone becoming a loyal brand advocate.

So, how do you find your "why"? Here are some questions to think about:
- What impact do I want my business to have on the world or my community?
- What personal experiences or passions led me to start this business?
- Beyond making money, what deeper purpose does my business serve?
- How do I want my customers to feel when they interact with my brand?
- What values are non-negotiable in how I conduct my business?

As you progress on our journey, you'll see that your "why" becomes the centerpiece of your story. Crafting a compelling narrative around it not only attracts customers but also potential investors and partners. They're not just investing in a product or service; they're investing in a vision, a mission, and a passion. So, take the time to dig deep and truly understand your "why". It'll be the guiding star for your business and the story you share with the world.

ACTIVITY

Finding Your Why

In this section, the questions being asked help us to identify the why of your business.

Origins:

What personal experiences or passions led me to start this business?

Impact:

What positive change do you want to bring about through your business?

Challenges:

What personal challenges have you overcome that led you to create this business?

Passions:

What are you deeply passionate about that's also related to your business?

Values:

What core values do you want your business to uphold, no matter what?

Legacy

How do you want your business to be remembered in the future?

Needs:

What unmet need in the market or community is your business addressing?

Emotions:

How do you want your customers to feel when they interact with your products or services?

Vision:

If your business succeeds in its ultimate goal, what will that world look like?

Differences:

How does your business approach problems or solutions differently from others?

Mission, Vision, And Elevtor Pitch

Now that you've dug deep and found out the heart of your business, it's time to get to the fun part: shaping what you'll sell and how you'll talk about it. We're going to craft a clear vision for your business, set out its mission, and then boil it all down into a snappy elevator pitch. Let's bring your ideas to life!

Components Of A Mission Statement

1. <u>Purpose</u>: Defines why the company exists and its primary objectives.
2. <u>Action</u>: Describes what the company does, typically in terms of products, services, and target audience.
3. <u>Values</u>: Highlights the core beliefs and principles that guide the company's actions and decisions.

Example:

"We empower creative minds by providing innovative tools, fostering an inclusive community, and championing sustainable practices."

Mission Statement Framework:

- Define Your Purpose: Start by asking yourself why your business exists. What problem are you solving or need are you addressing?
- Identify Your Actions: Detail what your business does to fulfill that purpose. What products or services do you offer? Who are they for?
- Highlight Your Values: Reflect on the principles that guide your business decisions. What are the non-negotiable values that underpin everything you do?
- Combine and Refine: Bring all these elements together into one cohesive statement. Keep it concise, clear, and powerful. It should resonate with both you and your target audience.

Remember, your mission statement is the compass for your business, guiding its direction and helping you stay true to your core purpose and values.

Now It's Your Turn:

Mission Statement

Vision Statement

Components Of A Vision Statement

1. <u>Future Orientation:</u> Describes where the company aspires to be in the future.
2. <u>Inspiration:</u> Provides a source of inspiration and motivation for those within and connected to the company.
3. <u>Guiding Principle</u>: Acts as a guide for setting goals, making decisions, and driving the company's growth.
4. <u>Clear and Concise</u>: While looking ahead, it should be succinct and easily understandable.

Example:

"To inspire and nurture the human spirit – one person, one cup, and one neighborhood at a time."

Vision Statement Framework:

1. **Visualize the Future**: Imagine where you want your company to be in 5, 10, or even 20 years. What impact has it made? What does it stand for?
2. **Identify Your Impact**: Think about the difference your company will make in the lives of its customers, community, or even the world.
3. **Align with Core Values**: Make sure that the vision aligns with the company's core values and beliefs.
4. **Be Concise and Specific**: Use clear and straightforward language. Your vision should be a beacon, easy for anyone to understand and get behind.

Remember, your vision statement sets the direction for your company's future and provides a long-term goal that everyone can work towards.

Now It's Your Turn:

Vision Statement

Elevator Pitch

Components Of An Elevator Pitch

1. <u>Introduction</u>: Briefly introduce yourself and your business.
2. <u>Problem Statement</u>: Clearly identify the problem or need your business addresses.
3. <u>Solution</u>: Describe how your product or service provides a solution to the identified problem.
4. <u>Unique Selling Proposition (USP)</u>: Highlight what makes your solution stand out from the competition.

Example:

"Hi, I'm Alex, founder of EcoDrink. Did you know that over 2 million plastic bottles are used every minute? Our solution, EcoDrink, offers biodegradable beverage containers that decompose in just 30 days. Unlike other products, ours are both heat-resistant and affordable."

Elevator Pitch Framework:

1. **Start with a Hook**: Begin with a compelling fact, question, or statement to grab attention.
2. **Identify the Problem**: Clearly articulate the issue your business addresses.
3. **Present Your Solution**: Describe your product or service and how it tackles the problem.
4. **Highlight Your USP**: Emphasize what sets your solution apart from others.

Remember, your elevator pitch should be concise and compelling, ideally lasting no longer than 30 seconds to a minute, capturing the essence of your business quickly and effectively.

Now It's Your Turn:

Elevator Pitch

Bringing It All Together: From beginning to Pitch

Your journey from the start of your business idea to crafting its voice is transformative. It's about connecting the dots:

Inception: This is where it all began, the birth of your idea. It's the "why" driving your passion and setting the foundation for everything that follows.

Vision Statement: Your vision paints a picture of the future, illustrating where you aspire to take your business. It's the North Star guiding your long-term aspirations.

Mission Statement: This defines your business's present. It's your day-to-day purpose, describing what you do, who you do it for, and the values you uphold.

Elevator Pitch: The culmination of all the above, put into a concise pitch. It's your business's introduction to the world, designed to capture attention and leave a lasting impression.

Each of these elements informs the next, creating a cohesive narrative for your business. They're like pieces of a puzzle, and when they fit together perfectly, they present a clear, compelling picture of who you are, what you stand for, and where you're headed.

As we transition into product development, remember that this foundation you've built will be crucial. It'll guide not just what you create, but how you present it to the world, ensuring alignment with your core purpose and values.

NOTES

NOTES

NOTES

Chapter 3

Understand the importance of identifying ideal customers to ensure business growth.

Determine and define who your customer will be, their desires, and interest.

Getting Started with Product Development

Now that we've laid the groundwork for your business, it's time to dive into product development. This is the exciting part where your ideas become real things people can use.

Product development is all about turning your vision into a real product or service. It's taking what you believe in and making something that your customers will love and find useful.

It's more than just making a thing; it's about making something that fits perfectly with what your business stands for. Whether it's a new gadget, an app, or a service, this is your chance to show the world what you've got.

Remember, the key to a great product is making sure it's not only useful but also true to your brand.

ACTIVITY

Diving into Product Development

Having set the stage for your business, we're now stepping into the exciting phase of product development. This is where your big ideas start to take shape and become actual products or services people can experience.

But before we dive in, take a moment to really think about what you're going to sell. Is it a tangible item, a digital tool, or maybe a unique service? It should be something that not only solves a problem but also connects with your brand's essence.

The Business will sell:	The Business will sell to:	The Business is located:
☐ Physical Product	☐ End consumer	☐ Website
☐ Physical Service	☐ Another Business	☐ Storefront
☐ Digital Product	☐ Both	☐ Warehouse
☐ Digital Service		☐ Home

Reflecting On Your Offering

Before we move ahead, let's pause and reflect:

- What is that one thing you believe your target audience truly needs?
- How does this product or service fit into the bigger picture of your business vision?
- Is it something you're passionate about and can stand behind?

Remember, the heart and soul of a great product or service line is in its ability to resonate with both your vision and your customers' needs. It's not just about filling a gap in the market; it's about filling it in a way that's unmistakably YOU.

Who are your target customers? Why them?

What are their needs that your product or service solves?

Why will customers want to buy from you?

Where can you reach your target customers?

What main pain points are you solving for your customers? What are you helping them achieve?

Mapping Your Product to Your Customer's Journey

Every product has a story, and every customer is on a journey. The magic happens when the two intersect. Now that you've shaped your product, it's important to imagine not just what you're selling, but who the people are that will buy into your vision- while serving their needs.

Imagine the customer's path. They might first hear about your product through a friend, or perhaps they stumble upon it while mindlessly scrolling through TikTok. Maybe they see an ad or read a review. Each of these touch points is an opportunity for you to present your product in a way that resonates with them.

Your product isn't just an item or a service; it's an experience. And the places you choose to sell – be it a physical store, an online marketplace, or even a community event – play a pivotal role in shaping that experience. As you continue develop your product, always keep the customer's journey in mind. Think about where they are, what they're looking for, and how you can make their path cross with your product in a meaningful way.

Ideal Customer Considerations:

What platforms do they use the most ? (Social Media etc.)	What websites do they use the most?

What kind of businesses do your ideal customer buy from?

What kind of media do they regularly use?
(Blogs, Videos, News, Podcast etc.)

What do they think about?	What are their interest?

What are their primary concerns in life? How does your product/service help to solve their concerns?

What are their main goals in life? How does your product/service help them fulfill their goals?

Final Thoughts

Starting a business is a journey filled with learning. You might start with a clear idea of who your customers are and what you want to sell them. But as you grow, you might notice some surprises.

For instance, let's say you plan to sell customized onesies for new moms. But as time goes on, you find out it's not just new moms buying them. Instead, many of your customers are friends or family shopping for a perfect gift for new moms. Suddenly, you're solving a different problem!

This is where marketing comes in. By watching who buys from you and listening to their feedback, you'll get clues. You'll understand better who loves your product and why.

Changes like this can be surprising, but they're also opportunities. They show you new paths to success.

In the upcoming chapters, we'll dive deeper into understanding your audience and fine-tuning your approach. But up next? We'll explore the best business model for you, setting you up for long term success.

Chapter 4

Discover your business model, lay the ground work for your business, and think about who will help you make it happen.

For our hands-on activity, we'll outline our business goals and determine the steps we need to take.

The Blueprint of Success: Business Models

Every building starts with a blueprint, and every business begins with a model. At its core, a business model is your game plan. It's the strategy you'll use to make money, outlining how your business will operate, attract customers, and generate profits.

Think of it like a roadmap. It shows you where you're going, how you'll get there, and what you'll need along the way. It defines what value you offer to customers and how you'll deliver that value efficiently. It's not just about selling a product or service; it's about understanding the entire ecosystem around it: from sourcing materials to delivering the final product and everything in between.

For business owners, the right model can make all the difference. It's the backbone that supports every decision, from day-to-day operations to long-term growth strategies. Without a clear business model, even the best ideas can struggle. But with the right one, even simple concepts can thrive.

Please don't confuse your business model with a business plan; it's your vision in action. It's crucial to take the time to get it right, ensuring that your business isn't just profitable, but sustainable and adaptable in a market that is constantly changing.

Key Considerations:

The upcoming activity is designed to prompt critical thinking. We'll be exploring questions that might seem simple on the surface, but they're the kind that can shape the destiny of your business. These are the questions that, when answered with care and insight, will lay a solid foundation for your business model.

Each question is a building block, helping you piece together a model that's not just viable but tailored to your unique vision and goals. By the end of this activity, you'll have a clearer understanding of how your business will operate, generate revenue, and thrive in the marketplace

Remember, the strength of your business model lies your ability to articulate to funders how you will be successful.

ACTIVITY

Business Goals:

Every journey needs a destination, and in business, that's your goal. It's the guiding light that shows you where you're headed. Having a clear business goal means you have direction. It helps you make decisions, prioritize tasks, and stay focused. Simply put, it's the big reason your business exists and what you hope to achieve.

What are your business goals?
(List top 5 goals)

What You Need to Start: Laying the Groundwork:

Before you begin any journey, you need the right tools and supplies. In business, knowing what you need to start ensures you're prepared. It helps you avoid surprises, plan your budget, and set the stage for smooth operations. Think of it as packing the essentials for a trip, making sure you're ready.

How will you get started?

Building a Strong Team

Every successful venture relies on a team, be it employees, key staff, or contractors. They're the people who help bring your vision to life. Having the right support means tasks get done efficiently, ideas get richer, and challenges become easier to overcome. It's like having a dependable crew on a ship, ensuring you sail smoothly towards your goal. You don't need to know their exact titles right now, but put down what you will need for them to help you do.

Who will offer you support?

Deciding to Hire or Outsource

You won't be able to wear every hat. There will be skills and expertise you'll need that may not be in your current repertoire. Identifying these skills early on helps you decide whether to hire in-house talent or outsource to specialists.

When considering hiring, think about:

- Longevity: Is this a skill you'll need consistently?
- Budget: Can you afford a full-time salary or would a contractor be more cost-effective?
- Control: Do you want this expertise closely integrated into your team?

Outsourcing can offer flexibility and specialized expertise, but hiring can bring in-house knowledge and cohesion.

For me, as an entrepreneur, this decision remains one of the trickier ones. Every business is unique, and what works for one might not work for another. It's a balance of understanding your needs, forecasting future demands, and considering the dynamics you want within your team.

What key skills must your team members have?

What key skills must your team members have?

Now What?

You're new to this, and it's normal not to know everything or everyone you need from the get-go. But here's the thing: you've got to start thinking about your team early on. Who do you need? Maybe someone who's great with numbers to handle the finances, or someone who's a master at marketing to get the word out about your business.

It's not unusual to assume many roles at first, but you are going to have to get over that QUICK!

To get comfortable with the idea of learning who will help you run your business, here is a list of local and global resources you can tap into that will help you do some research and when you're ready-hire.

Hiring Locally and Internationally

When it comes to finding these people, there are tons of websites out there where you can find talent, both in your own backyard and across the globe. These sites let you see what people charge for their work, what kind of job titles they have (which can be super helpful when you're new to this), and even save a list of potential team members for when you're ready to hire.

1. **LinkedIn** - Great for professional networking and finding people with the skills you need.
2. **Upwork** - Perfect for finding freelancers from around the world for all sorts of jobs.
3. **Indeed** - A job board where you can post jobs and find candidates locally.
4. **Glassdoor** - Useful for getting an idea of what salaries are like and reading company reviews.
5. **Fiverr** - Good for finding freelancers for smaller, specific tasks.
6. **Freelancer.com** - Another spot for finding freelance talent worldwide.
7. **Monster** - A traditional job search website where you can find a wide range of candidates.
8. **Remote.co** - If you're open to hiring people to work remotely, this is a great place to look.
9. **AngelList** - If your business is a startup, this site is a good place to find people interested in startup culture.
10. **Craigslist** - Good for local hires and a wide variety of job postings.

Reminder:

While you're browsing these sites, keep an open mind. You might stumble upon jobs or skills that you didn't even know you needed. Maybe there's someone who specializes in social media, which could be super useful for getting the word out about your business. Or perhaps you find someone who's a pro at web design, which could be crucial for your online presence.

Remember, building a business is a lot like putting together a puzzle. You need all the right pieces—and people—to complete the picture. So take your time, do your research, and start building a list of potential team members who can help you reach that destination.

Additional Resources:

We spent an entire month talking about hiring, firing onboarding, selecting talent, and all the steps you will need to take when the time comes. You are free to check out these five impactful episodes that will help you string all of the pieces together.

*Photos are linked for e-book

Up Next: Understanding Your Market

NOTES

NOTES

NOTES

Chapter 5

This chapter is all about create a product to client fit that will dominate the market.

For our hands-on activity, we're going to tie in all the elements of your product and ideal customer.

Welcome to a pivotal chapter in your entrepreneurial journey—Product/Service Research. As you stand at the threshold of carving a niche for your business, it's essential to dive deep into the realm of research. This isn't just any step; it's the compass that will guide your venture towards your ultimate destination.

Where You'll Sell: Matching Your Product to Your Customer

Imagine setting sail without a map. That's what venturing into business without research is like. For black women in business, who are crafting their unique narratives in the marketplace, understanding the intricacies of product/service research is not just beneficial—it's your entire business.

Research is the foundation upon which your business will stand. It's about knowing the terrain before you step onto it. It's about understanding not just the 'what' but the 'why' of your product or service. Why does it matter? Why will it resonate with your audience? Why will it outshine the competition?

The Market Landscape: Know What Exists

Do you know what they need? This is where you turn your gaze outward—to the market. What's already out there? What's working, and what's not?

The importance of knowing the existing market cannot be overstated. It's like knowing the other players on the chessboard. You see, the market is a conversation, and to be heard, you must first listen. What are customers praising? What are they complaining about? These are the whispers that can become your shout.

Learning From The Competition: A Mirror To Your Success

Your competitors are not just rivals; they're unintentional mentors. They've laid out a blueprint—what to do and what not to do. By exploring what they offer, you're not just gathering intelligence; you're gathering inspiration.

What are people loving about your competitors' products? What are they criticizing? This is invaluable feedback, and it's free. It's a window into the consumer's mind. Can you improve upon what's being offered? Is there a gap that's not being filled? This is your cue.

Innovate and Elevate: Adding Your Unique Touch

Now comes the fun part. Innovation. What can you bring to the table that's not already there? Think of your product/service as a canvas. Your competitors might have the basic colors, but you? You're going to bring the entire spectrum.

Maybe it's a service feature that saves time, or a product enhancement that adds value. For example, if you're in the beauty industry and notice that customers want more sustainable options, could you introduce eco-friendly packaging? If you're in tech, and there's a cry for better customer service, could you offer round-the-clock support?

Remember, it's not just about adding features for the sake of it. It's about adding value. It's about understanding that this is still part of sculpting your business model—a model that stands on the pillars of what your customers cherish and what the market lacks.

As you embark on this research journey, remember that it's a continuous process. It's about staying agile, staying informed, and staying ahead. This isn't just a chapter in your businesses plans; it's a chapter in your story. A story that you're telling one research point at a time.

So, take this knowledge, make it your own, and let it guide you to a business that's not just built on dreams, but on deliberate, data-driven decisions. Welcome to the world of informed entrepreneurship. Welcome to the future of your business.

ACTIVITY

Let's dive into a market discovery adventure, identifying customer desires, analyzing rivals, and crafting standout features to elevate our business blueprint.

Product or Service:	

Note: This should only be conducted for one product at a time. If you need additional pages or additional products, I will add them at the back of the book.

Customer motivation to buy the proposed solution.

Top 3 similar products sold and their features

Top 3 similar products sold and the features their missing

What features could you offer that can add value?

How to decide the most important features

In a busy business marketplace, our mission is clear: to crate a product that speaks directly to the heart of our customers' needs. We begin by listening intently to what the market is asking for—the frustrations and wishes of those we will ultimately serve. Each feature we consider is a potential key to solving their most pressing needs.

We look over feedback and reviews like a detective, looking for patterns and clues. What are customers missing? What do they hope for? Our feature list becomes a reflection of their voices, each feature promising to fill a gap in the make up of the current offerings.

You need to understand that not all features are created equal. We have to weigh them, balancing the scales of impact against the effort. We ask ourselves, "Which features carry the torch of innovation further, faster, and more efficiently?" These become what guides our decisions.

Each feature must be in harmony with our customers' needs but also align with the goals of our business. We prototype, we test, we iterate—each step a stitch in the ultimate make up of our product's story.

And so, with a map drawn from data, customer insight, and strategic foresight, we can build a successful product. The features we choose to prioritize are more than just functions; they are commitments to our customers, pillars of our brand, and the milestones on our journey to success.

Measuring the priority:

In our efforts to innovate, we introduce an important: the Priority Matrix. This tool is what I use for guidance, allows us to travel through a sea of potential features. It's not just about what we could do; it's about what we should do.

As we gather around this matrix, you will plot your product's features at the cross of customer value and your effort. Those that prioritize high value to it's users and low effort on our part are the ideal products.

I want you to think of yourself as more than just a creator; you're a strategist. The Priority Matrix helps us discern which features will be our champions—those that deliver maximum impact with a manageable investment of our resources. It's a dance of cost versus benefit, effort versus reward.

Features that land in the quadrant of high value and high effort are aspirational. We may not scale them today, but they will stay at top of our minds , reminding us of what we hope to one day achieve and what we're working towards.

Features that map out as low value, regardless of effort, are the ones we release. They may be interesting, but they don't serve our us in being distinctive in the eyes of our customers.

This matrix is a tool; and it's a testament to our commitment to serve with laser sharp precision, to build with purpose, and to prioritize with the wisdom of the market's demands.

Measuring The Priority: The Matrix

Leverage this worksheet to identify key client-desired features and evaluate their implementation and complexity, providing clear direction on feature prioritization for your product or service. You will do this for every product. Additional sheets are in the back

Product One:

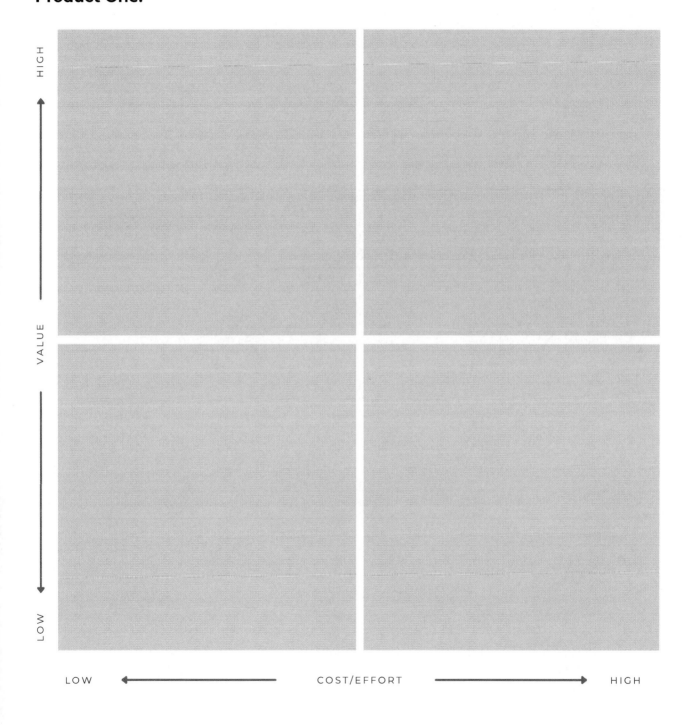

Product Two:

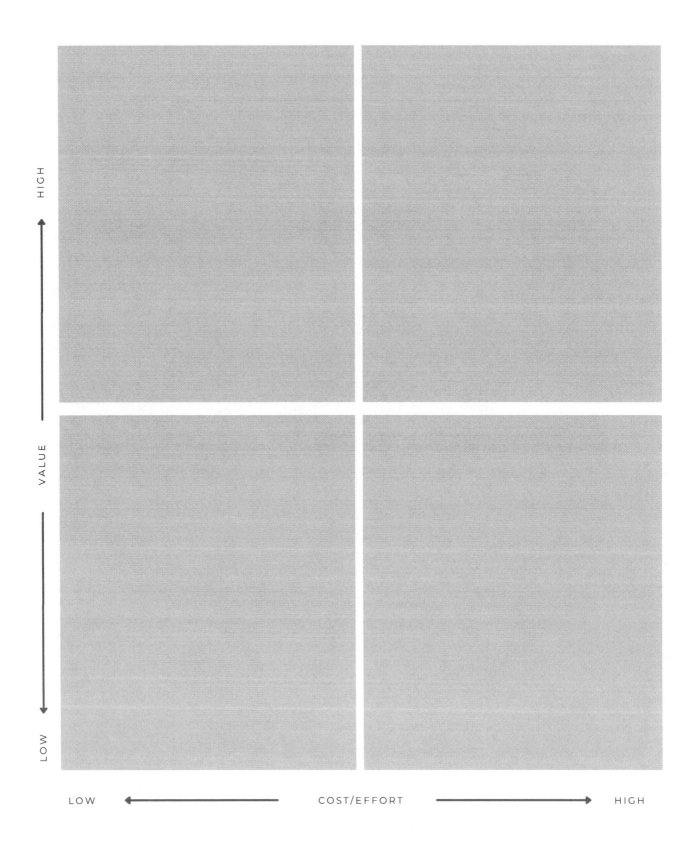

HIGH

VALUE

LOW

LOW   COST/EFFORT   HIGH

Product Three:

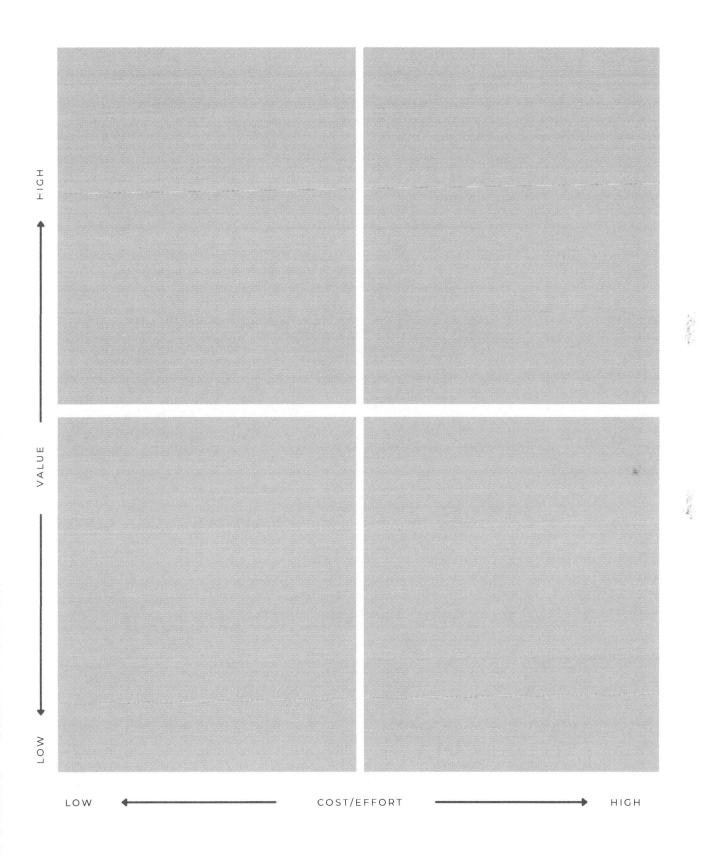

Product Four:

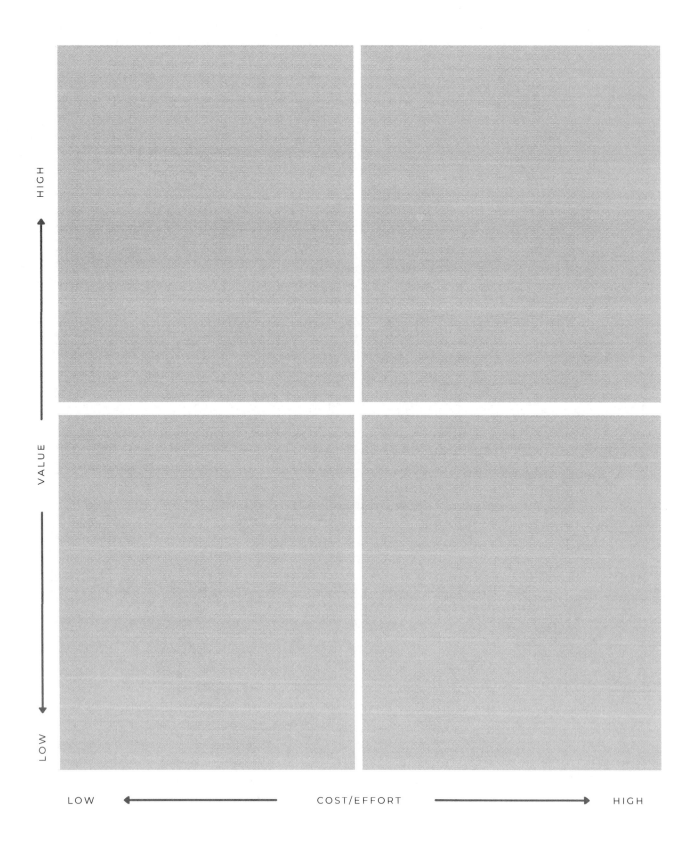

HIGH

VALUE

LOW

LOW ⟵ COST/EFFORT ⟶ HIGH

Product Five:

HIGH

VALUE

LOW

LOW ← COST/EFFORT → HIGH

Competitors: A Deeper Look

Now we talk about competition. Competition is not just a challenge; it's an opportunity—a chance to outshine and outperform. The stage is set, and the players are household names like Tide and Gain, each with a loyal audience that goes with their every move. But how does a new entrant into the market capture the spotlight and turn the audience's attention away from what they have already fallen in-love with?

The goal is not to just move attention away from tried-and-true favorites; it's to create a performance so compelling that it draws eyes naturally. Customers have their loyalties, but they also cant help themselves when new things come into the market in hopes of something better, something that resonates with their evolving needs and desires.

Your role is to become a student of your competition. Study Tide's formula for success—what methods of trust and efficiency have they infused into their brand story? Pay attention to Gain's variety of fragrances—how do they create that perfect harmony that resonates with their users?

But while you're looking, look for the subtle notes of discord—the faint dissatisfaction. What do customers wish was different? What features are they silently wishing for? This is where your opportunity lies. This is your cue to innovate.

Take what's good and make it your own; then take what's lacking and make it your highlight. If Tide's strength is cleaning power, match that, but if some yearn for eco-friendliness, make that your strength. If Gain's fragrance is alluring but its longevity is not long enough for customers, ensure your product not only sings a similar aromatic tune but also carries the notes longer.

This strategic method is not a one-act play; it's a strategy that unfolds with each market shift, each trend, each new desire. Revisit your competitive analysis regularly—monthly, or at the very least, quarterly. Keep your script updated, your performance fresh, and your audience engaged.

Remember, in this market theater, your business is not just a show; it's a narrative that you continuously rewrite, always aiming to captivate the audience more profoundly than the act before.

Your Competition

List three of the people who already do what you want to do well. If you dont think there is anything in your industry, you still need to do this exercise. The new entrants into the market will be assessing your business to determine what they are competing against. If you dont think you have competition, the compeition is the company who would be doing what you're doing perfectly. Get creative. (The additional compeitiors pages will be in the back of the book.

Primary Competition

What problems do they solve?

What is your competition really good at?

Where is there room for improvement?

What do they do to reach their target audience?

Where do they go to reach their target audience?

How are they pricing their products?

Pricing Strategy

As we turn our attention to a pricing strategy, we're not just setting a number; we're defining value. Pricing is a language that communicates your product's worth to the consumer and it's place in the competitive landscape.

The right price is a blend of art and science. It's a strategic decision that can propel your product to success or cast it into the shadows. To navigate this, you have to do some more research.

Let's look the pricing landscape. How has your competition structured their pricing? (I'm about to throw some jargon at you, but I will explain, I promise.) Are they using cost-plus pricing, adding a standard markup to the cost of the products? Maybe they've adopted value-based pricing, aligning the price with the perceived value to the customer. Or are they playing the game of competitive pricing, setting prices based on what the rest of the market is doing?

Your pricing strategy should not be a mirror reflection but a calculated response. If Tide prices premium, is it because of brand perception, or does the product genuinely offer a superior clean? If Gain opts for penetration pricing, is it to quickly capture market share?

Now, look inward. What are your costs? What is the unique value you offer? Your pricing must cover your costs and then some, to be sure you can be profitable. But it must also resonate with the perceived value your customers place on your product.

Consider psychological pricing; maybe pricing just below a round number can influence perception. Think about bundle pricing if it increases the perceived value. And don't forget about promotional pricing, which can be a strategic move to draw attention and disrupt loyal customer bases.

As you sculpt your pricing strategy, remember that it is fluid. Test, learn, and be ready to adapt. Your price is a powerful tool—not just to cover costs or generate profit, but to send a clear message to the market about who you are and the value you bring.

URGENT

NO MATTER WHAT YOU DO, PLEASE DO NOT BASE YOUR PRICES ON BEING THE LOWEST IN THE MARKET, YOU WILL BE PRICED OUT.

Pricing Strategy Examples

Cost-Plus Pricing	Penetration Pricing	Value-Based Pricing
This involves adding a markup to the cost of producing a product. If a t-shirt costs $5 to make, you might sell it for $15, marking up the price by $10.	Setting a low initial price to attract customers and gain market share. A new streaming service offers a discounted rate for the first 6 months.	Price based on perceived product value to customers. Organic skincare priced high due to perceived quality.
Competitive Pricing	Skimming Pricing	Psychological Pricing
Set prices based on competitor pricing strategies. Set prices based on competitor pricing strategies.	High initial price for new, innovative products. Launching a new tech gadget at a premium price.	Pricing that considers the psychology of numbers. Pricing an item at $1.99 instead of $2
Bundle Pricing	Premium Pricing:	Economy Pricing
Selling a set of products for a lower total cost. Three for the price of two special shampoo offer.	Keeping prices high to encourage a luxury brand image. Designer handbags priced to denote exclusivity.	Very low pricing, minimal marketing costs, aimed at sensitivity. Generic medication priced lower than branded products.

Additional Resources:

We spent an entire month talking about pricing from nearly every angle you janimagine. I still revisit these episodes when I need clarity. These 4 episodes outline the steps you will need to take when it comes to pricing . You are free to check out these four impactful episodes that will help you string all of the pieces together.

*Photos are linked for e-book

Competitor Pricing Strategy

Now that you know what some of the options are (there are a ton more so if you don't see it on this list, search for other pricing strategies), its time to look at what strategy they use as it could inform your strategy.

How does your competition price their products? What strategy are they using?

S. W. O. T

SWOT analysis is a strategic planning tool that stands for Strengths, Weaknesses, Opportunities, and Threats. It's a framework for assessing these four aspects of your business, product, or project.

Strengths: Characteristics of the business or project that give it an advantage over others.
Weaknesses: Characteristics that place your business at a disadvantage relative to other businesses in your industry.
Opportunities: Elements that the project/ business could exploit to its advantage.
Threats: Elements in the environment that could cause problems for the business or project.

Conducting a SWOT analysis is important because it provides a clear picture of where your business or project currently stands and what potential it has to grow or face challenges. It's a foundational step in strategy development, ensuring that you're aware of your internal capabilities and external possibilities, and ready to take on any obstacles.

For the next activity you are going to conduct a S.W.O.T analysis for your top two compeititons and for yourself. You need to understand how you measure up, where there is room for improvement, and what you can leverage to get people to want to use your product and service.

ACTIVITY

Employ this SWOT Analysis template to identify your competitive advantages, areas for improvement, potential prospects, and possible risks. It will guide you to prioritize strategic initiatives and steer clear of potential setbacks.

S.W.O.T Analysis: Competitor 1

Competitor Name	

STRENGTHS	WEAKNESSES

OPPORTUNITIES	THREATS

S.W.O.T Analysis: Competitor 2

Competitor Name	

STRENGTHS	WEAKNESSES

OPPORTUNITIES	THREATS

S.W.O.T Analysis: Your Company

Your Name	

STRENGTHS	WEAKNESSES
OPPORTUNITIES	**THREATS**

Products & Features

Last but absolutely not least, we will be examining the features that you will be putting into your prodcut or service. You will use all of the information you gathered and make informed decisions about what is most important to your ideal consumer, what features your product will have, and at the strategy you will use to price your product or service at. I added additional boxes so that you can do this for multiple products if you have them already in mind.

Product 1:

Product/ Service	
KEY FEATURES	PRICING STRATEGY AND PRICE

Product 2:

Product/ Service

KEY FEATURES	PRICING STRATEGY AND PRICE

Notes:

Product 3:

Product/ Service

KEY FEATURES	PRICING STRATEGY AND PRICE

Notes:

Product 4:

Product/ Service

KEY FEATURES	PRICING STRATEGY AND PRICE

Notes:

Product 5:

Product/ Service

KEY FEATURES	PRICING STRATEGY AND PRICE

Notes:

As we close the chapter on market analysis, competition, and pricing strategies, we've armed ourselves with a deep understanding of the battlefield we're stepping into. We've dissected the strengths that will be our sword, the weaknesses we must shield, the opportunities we shall seize, and the threats we must be wary of. We've also navigated the intricate web of pricing, ensuring our tags speak the language of value and strategy.

Now, it's time to turn the page. The next chapter challenges us to a new but equally important element—Client Acquisition. Here, we will unravel the 'how' of bringing your product or service to your clients. We'll explore the channels, the messages, and the tactics that will bridge the gap between what you offer and those who need it most. So, take a deep breath and prepare to dive into the art and science of capturing the hearts and minds of your future customers.

INDEPTH SWOT ANALYSIS TRAINING

Ready to revolutionize your strategic planning with SWOT analysis? Unlock your organization's potential, tackle weaknesses, seize opportunities, and shield against threats. Our dynamic training equips you with the tools to make impactful decisions and steer your company towards success. Don't miss out on the chance to become a strategic mastermind. Secure your spot in our in-depth SWOT analysis training now!

NOTES

NOTES

NOTES

Chapter 6

OBJECTIVE

Discover how to bring attention to your brand, map out how you will get it done and get the tools you need to do it.

ACTIVITY

For our hands-on activity, we'll go deep into the tools that get customers in the door and the marketing tools that make it happen.

Bringing Awareness: Letting People Know You're Here

Chapter 6 ushers us into the world of marketing. With a clear picture of our customer, their preferences, the right price point, and our competitive edge, the next pivotal step is to ensure that our product or service becomes a known choice for our customers.

In this introduction to marketing, we lay the groundwork for more intricate strategies to come. Our focus here is to craft a narrative that resonates with potential funders and donors, one that underscores the thoughtfulness and efficacy of our approach.

We'll delve into the channels used by our target audience, the messaging that aligns with their values and needs, and the timing that could maximize our impact. We'll think about the digital footprints we create through social media, the partnerships that could amplify our reach, and the storytelling that will make our brand unforgettable.

This chapter is not about tactics; it's about setting the stage for them. It's about making sure that when we speak to those who will support our journey financially, we provide a clear, strategic vision of how we plan to connect with the hearts and wallets of our customers.

So, as we navigate this chapter, let's keep our end goal in sight: to lay a solid foundation for marketing strategies that not only resonate with our audience but also inspire confidence in those who invest in our vision.

What is a marketing strategy?

A marketing strategy is a comprehensive plan curated by a business to reach prospective consumers and turn them into customers of their products or services. It outlines the company's value proposition, key brand messaging, data on target customer demographics, and other high-level elements. The strategy provides a blueprint for reaching marketing goals, such as increasing brand awareness or market penetration, and is typically structured around the following components:

1. **Market Research**: Understanding the market dynamics, customer needs, and preferences, and the competitive landscape. Which we've already done.
2. **Target Audience**: Identifying and profiling the segment of the market that the business intends to serve. Which we've already done.
3. **Positioning**: Defining how the product or service fits into the market and how it is distinct from competitors. Which we've already done.
4. **Marketing Mix (9 Ms)**: Money, Merchandise, Market, Methods, Message, Medium, Mindshare, Mates, and Mechanics strategies that will be used to reach and appeal to the target market. Which we're about to do.
5. **Goals and Objectives**: Specific, measurable, achievable, relevant, and time-bound (SMART) goals that the business aims to achieve through its marketing efforts. Which we're about to do.
6. **Budget**: The financial plan for the marketing strategy, detailing how much money will be allocated to each marketing activity. Which you have to consider at some point.
7. **Channels and Tactics**: The specific methods and platforms (such as social media, email marketing, content marketing, etc.) that will be used to communicate with and engage the target audience. Which we're about to do.
8. **Measurement and Analysis**: The metrics that will be used to evaluate the effectiveness of marketing activities and the process for collecting and analyzing this data. Which which you have to consider at some point.

A successful marketing strategy is one that is well-researched, data-driven, and flexible enough to adapt to market changes. It aligns with your company's broader business goals and is consistently reviewed and refined based on performance metrics and market/ customer feedback.

What is a marketing strategy?

We've already covered some of the M's so in the activity we are going to block out the ones that are not relevant to us (Merchandise/ Product, Money/ Price, Mates/ Hiring, just as a few examples)

Embarking on the 6 M's Marketing Matrix, we're set to navigate through a comprehensive framework that will shape our marketing strategy with meticulous precision. This activity will immerse us in the realms of Money, Merchandise, Methods, and others.

We'll evaluate our **Money** strategy to be sure that pricing reflects our brand's value, dissect our **Merchandise** to showcase its distinct features, understand our **Market** to genuinely connect with our audience, develop **Methods** that engage and convert, craft our **Message** to captivate and inspire, select the **Medium** that best delivers our content, build **Mindshare** to secure a prominent place in consumer consciousness, choose **Mates** who will strengthen and reflect our vision, and refine our **Mechanics** to ensure seamless operations.

This matrix is our map to a marketing strategy that's not only coherent but also resonates deeply with our target audience, guiding us toward achieving our overarching business goals. As we delve into each 'M', let's approach with an analytical mindset and innovative spirit, ready to construct a marketing structure that's robust.

ACTIVITY

We're going to explore each area of the Mental Money Marketing Matrix, why it's important and then you'll get a chance to unpack how this will impact your business/ ability to articulate success to funders.

M-One: Methods

'Methods' encapsulates the diverse array of tactics and procedures a business employs to reach its objectives. This includes the execution plans for product launches, customer engagement techniques, sales tactics, and after-sales service. It's about the 'how' in the journey from product development to customer satisfaction—choosing the right mix of strategies to create a seamless and effective path to market success.

What will you need to do to market your product or service?

Marketing Activities

I will share with you ideas of the marketing activities that you can use as a method to get your product or service in front of your audience. These are the ones that I have seen work historically, especially if you have an online business, however, if I were you, I would look to my industry to see what the industry standard is.

Sales Funnels

Think of a sales funnel as a guide that helps people learn about a problem they have and shows them how to fix it. It's like answering the big questions they might type into Google or ask someone they trust.

You create different kinds of helpful information (like the steps in our funnel model) to lead them step by step. They start by learning about their problem, then they discover all the ways to solve it, and by the end, they see why your solution is the best choice.

The funnel is also your chance to show you know your stuff and can be trusted. So make sure all the info you share is really useful and something people would want to read or download!

Funnel Phases

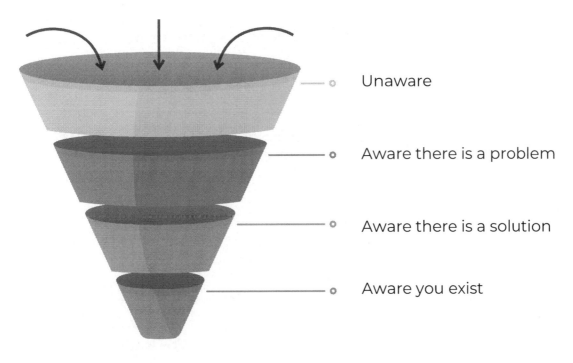

Unaware

Aware there is a problem

Aware there is a solution

Aware you exist

Ready to buy

Content Marketing

Content marketing is one way to get people into your funnel. You can create content for every phase of where they are. This allows them to feel seen heard and know that your solution is trusted. At each phase of the funnel you are speaking to your target customer differently and you will have different offerings for them. The content you produce will help to communicate what the next phase is, but ALWAYS leading them to ultimately purchase.

Sales Funnels

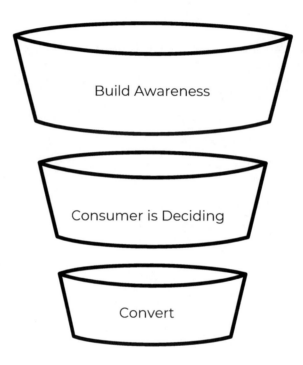

Build Awareness

Consumer is Deciding

Convert

Top of Funnel

This kind of content you create at the top helps people learn about your business. It's all about giving them useful stuff like blog posts that answer their big questions, how-to guides, fun videos, and useful tips on social media. It's there to help them figure out "How can I fix my problem?"

Middle of Funnel

This kind of content you create at the middle should be real-life examples and freebies, like a PDF they can download, to show why your stuff is worth it. They'll share their email or contact info to get it. This answers "Why should I get this from you?"

Bottom of Funnel

At the bottom of the sales or marketing funnel, the focus is on converting leads or prospects into paying customers. This is the stage where potential customers have progressed through the earlier stages of the funnel, such as awareness and interest, and are now close to making a purchase decision.

Bridging the Gap: Content Creation for Your Sales Funnel

I know for many of us the idea of creating content is challenging, but it's a necessary evil. Let's be clear even a business brochure is content. Whether you are on social media or now you will have to produce materials that explain who you are. Grant applications are no exception. The reason you are even reading this is because I generated content to get you aware of what you will need to develop in your business to position your business for funding, help provide the solution that ultimately influenced your buying decision.

Content within a sales funnel serves multiple purposes. It educates, engages, builds trust, and ultimately, persuades. Each stage of your sales funnel - awareness, interest, decision, and action - requires a different content approach to move a prospect to the next level effectively.

- Awareness: At this stage, your content should focus on addressing the initial problems or needs of your target market. It's about getting their attention with valuable information that resonates with their pain points or aspirations.

- Interest: Here, you delve deeper, showcasing your expertise and the uniqueness of your product or service. The content should make them consider your brand as a viable solution to their needs.

- Decision: Content at this stage should help overcome objections and answer any lingering questions. It's about providing proof points, like case studies, testimonials, or product demos, that reassure the buyer.

- Action: Finally, the content should encourage taking the final step - whether it's making a purchase, signing up for a service, or another call to action. It should be clear, compelling, and make the process as simple as possible.

Creating The Right Content

To be sure you're reaching the right people with the right message, you will need to make several considerations. Your content will need to be:

- **Relevant**: Tailor your content to address the specific concerns and desires of your target audience.
- **Valuable**: Offer insights, solutions, or entertainment that your audience cannot easily find elsewhere.
- **Consistent**: Maintain a steady flow of content to keep your audience engaged and to reinforce your message.
- **Actionable**: Every piece of content should have a clear next step for the audience to take.

Where you place the content and who you are targeting will depend on where they are in the funnel. The same messaging at the top of funnel is not the same messages at the bottom of funnel.

Just to be clear, this is not meant for you to take action today. There are a few more considerations you will need to make. The most important takeaway is that you need to understand these elements when communicating with funders your plan to get your name out there. This is going to be a blueprint, you dont have to start construction today.

Content Ideas : Top of Funnel

Top-of-funnel (TOFU) content is designed to attract and engage potential customers who are at the beginning of their buying journey. The goal at this stage is to create awareness and educate your audience about a problem or opportunity they may not have fully recognized yet. Here are some effective TOFU content ideas:

Educational Post	Infographics	Ebooks
Whitepapers	**Podcast**	**Checklist**

Content Ideas : Middle of Funnel

Middle-of-funnel (MOFU) content targets potential customers who are already aware of their problem or opportunity and are now considering the various solutions available. This stage is about nurturing leads, building trust, and positioning your product or service as the optimal solution. Here are some MOFU content ideas:

Case Studies	Testimonials	FAQ's
Webinar	How-To Guide	Workshops

Content Ideas : Bottom of Funnel

Bottom-of-funnel (BOFU) content is aimed at prospects who are on the verge of making a purchase decision. They've recognized their problem, considered the available solutions, and are now evaluating the best choice. BOFU content should help remove any last-minute doubts, answer final questions, and provide that final nudge to convert prospects into customers. Here are some BOFU content ideas:

Free-trial	Consultations	Discounts
Live Demos & Walkthroughs	Implementation Guide	Customer Success Stories

NOTE:

This is just a reminder that at the end of the day, this is a small list. There are a ton of activities that you can engage in that can help you nurutre relationships at all points of the funnel. The ultimate goal is go get clients in the door. Keeping them in the door is more of an advanced proposition, however, telling funders your plan to keep people coming into your business is a key element of funding.

What kind of content makes the most sense for your business. What will it be about?

What Top of Funnel actives will you engage into create awareness?

What Middle of Funnel actives will you engage into create awareness?

What Bottom of Funnel actives will you engage into create awareness?

As we've meticulously crafted content tailored for each stage of the sales funnel, the next important step is to ensure that this content reaches our audience. The platforms we choose for distribution are the conduits that connect our message with our potential customers. It's not just about where the content lives; it's about where our audience lives, works, and plays in the digital world.

Choosing the Right Platforms for Content Distribution

The platforms for distributing content should be as carefully considered as the content itself. They are the stages on which our content performs, and each has its own audience, culture, and set of expectations.

Social Media

Platforms like LinkedIn, Twitter, Facebook, and Instagram offer a direct line to consumers and businesses alike. They are the marketplaces where conversations happen and opinions form. For top-of-funnel content, these platforms are invaluable for building awareness and sparking interest. As we move to the middle of the funnel, these same platforms allow us to engage more deeply with our audience through targeted posts, ads, and direct engagement.

Your Website

Your website acts as your digital storefront. It's where interested prospects come to learn more after an initial encounter with your brand. Here, middle-of-funnel content can shine, providing deeper insights and convincing narratives through blog posts, articles, and videos. As for the bottom of the funnel, your website should facilitate a seamless transition to purchase or contact with clear calls-to-action and persuasive product pages.

Email Marketing

Email remains one of the most personal forms of digital communication. It allows us to reach into the inboxes of our audience with tailored messages. Drip campaigns can nurture leads through the funnel, delivering targeted content that addresses the recipient's stage in the buyer's journey.

Content Hubs and Publications

Publishing on established content hubs or industry publications can lend credibility and reach a wider audience. These platforms are excellent for distributing thought leadership pieces and in-depth analyses that can attract and influence decision-makers.

Video Platforms

Platforms like YouTube are not just for entertainment; they're educational powerhouses where detailed product demos and testimonials can live, providing a rich, visual experience for those in the decision-making phase.

Paid Advertising

Paid channels, such as PPC campaigns on Google or sponsored content on social media, can amplify the reach of your content, pushing it in front of those who are actively searching for solutions.

Partnerships and Influencers

Collaborating with influencers or complementary businesses can extend the reach of your content to new, relevant audiences. These partnerships can be particularly effective for distributing top-of-funnel content that requires a broad reach.

The Concept:

Imagine each piece of content as a traveler setting out on a journey to find its audience. Social media posts, like club prompters, venture out to create initial awareness. Your website acts as a home, where more detailed content resides, ready to offer shelter and information to those seeking it. Email campaigns are like messengers, delivering personalized and timely content directly to the hands of the audience. Content hubs and industry publications serve as the locals, proclaiming your message far and wide. Video platforms act as theaters, showing the visual stories of your brand. Paid advertising works as billboards, catching the eye of people passing by, while partnerships and influencers are like friends, introducing your content to new circles.

In this digital ecosystem, content must not only be well-crafted but also well-placed. The right content in the wrong place may as well be invisible. Therefore, our strategy is to place our content where our audience will naturally find it, engage with it, and act upon it. This is the art and science of content distribution, and it's where the magic of conversion happens. As we move forward, we'll align our distribution channels with our content types and funnel stages to ensure that our message not only reaches our audience but resonates with them, too.

M-Two: Medium

When considering where to push your content, it's vital to start with platforms that are industry-specific. These channels are frequented by your target audience and stakeholders who have a vested interest in your niche. By focusing on industry-specific forums, publications, and social media groups, you can ensure that your content is reaching the right eyes and ears—those who are most likely to engage with your message and move through your sales funnel.

If you're unsure about where to begin or hesitant to go into untested waters, these industry-specific platforms provide a solid foundation. They are the tried-and-true platform where your peers and potential customers are already active and engaged.

Distribution is undeniably a numbers game. When it comes to securing funding, investors want to see that you're not only reaching a wide audience but also engaging with them effectively. It's about demonstrating the ability to convert content views into leads, and leads into customers. This is where analytics and measurement come into play. By tracking the performance of your content across different channels, you can determine which ones yield the best return on investment.

Investing time or resources into a distribution channel without understanding its effectiveness is like sailing without a compass. You need to know what works and what doesn't. This data-driven approach will not only impress potential funders with hard numbers but also guide your strategy, helping you to allocate resources to the channels that contribute most to your funnel's success.

In the landscape of content distribution, there must be a balance between innovation and tradition. On one hand, it's important to leverage proven channels that have historically performed well within your industry. These are the platforms where your audience expects to find you, and where they're prepared to engage with your content.

Innovation should not be overlooked. The digital world is constantly changing, and new platforms can offer untapped opportunities to reach and engage with your audience in unique ways. Whether it's through emerging social media platforms, new content formats, or unconventional partnerships, being open to innovation can differentiate your brand and capture the attention of both customers and funders.

As we consider the distribution channels for your content, remember that each platform serves as a touchpoint in the customer journey—a chance to influence and persuade. Your choices should be strategic, data-informed, and reflective of a balance between what is proven and what is possible. By doing so, you'll not only fill your sales funnel with qualified leads but also build a compelling case for why funders should back your journey.

Selling Options

☐ **Direct to Consumer** _____

☐ **Use a Distributor** _____

☐ **Partner with a Store** _____

☐ **Use an Affiliate Program** _____

☐ **Dropshipping** _____

☐ **Whitelabel** _____

☐ **Other** _____

Where to Sell in Person

- [ ] Retail Store
- [ ] Pop-up Store
- [ ] Physical Market
- [ ] Partner with a Store
- [ ] Fairs & Conventions
- [ ] Kiosks
- [ ] Sell from Home
- [ ] Local Business Directories

- [ ] _____
- [ ] _____
- [ ] _____
- [ ] _____
- [ ] _____
- [ ] _____
- [ ] _____
- [ ] _____

Where to Sell Online

- [ ] Etsy Store
- [ ] Amazon Marketplace
- [ ] Ebay Auctions
- [ ] Print on Demand
- [ ] Facebook Marketplace
- [ ] Your Website
- [ ] Walmart Marketplace

- [ ] _____
- [ ] _____
- [ ] _____
- [ ] _____
- [ ] _____
- [ ] _____
- [ ] _____

Ecommerce Platforms

Shopify	BigCommerce	Magneto	Woocommerce

Social Media Platforms

Instagram Shopping	Pinterest

Specialty Platforms

Reverb	Postmark	ThredUP

Business To Business Platform

Alibaba	ThomasNet	Tradeshows

Digital Services

Gumroad	Upwork	Udemy

Subscription Model

Cratejoy	Subbly

Print On Demand

Printful	Rerubble

Every platform has their benefits and other have their downsides. Before you decide to marry a platform that you want to commit too, I would suggest looking at each and assessing which one is better and why. Also consider if your competition is using it too. All of these factors will allow you to weigh the best choice.

Where to Sell	Upside	Downside	What Platforms Do My Competitors Use?

The Part We All Hate, But Have To Do- Sales

In this section I am going to introduce you to a concept called AIDA. Once you learn it and master it, you will not be able to unsee it. It is everywhere and all good sellers use it. As a matter of fact I am using it right now in this paragah. You will use this framework for selling to your clients, attracting interest to your business in the form of funding, and to get people "glued" to what you have to say. I know you cant wait until you get to the point in your business where people are pouring money into your business because you've mastered the art of AIDA. Once you've used it and understand how powerful it is, you'll never NOT use it.

What is AIDA?

AIDA is an acronym that stands for Attention, Interest, Desire, and Action. It is a classic marketing and sales framework that drives the process of attracting and persuading potential customers. Let's break down each element of the framework and then talk about its relevance in the context of seeking funding for your journey:

ATTENTION	INTEREST
This is the stage where you need to grab the prospects attention. You can do this by creating a compelling elevator pitch or a visually engaging presentation that highlights the uniqueness of your journey or project. Use attention-grabbing headlines, visuals, or anecdotes to make your project stand out.	Once you have their attention, you need to pique their interest. Share information about your journey that makes it exciting and relevant to the investor. Explain the problem or challenge you are addressing and how your project offers a solution or opportunity. Use storytelling techniques to make your journey relatable and engaging.
DESIRE	ACTION
In this stage, you want to build a sense of desire or need for your journey in the minds of your potential funders. Clearly communicate the benefits and value your journey offers. Highlight the potential returns on investment, both in terms of financial gains and the impact your journey can make. Showcase your passion and commitment to make them want to be a part of your journey.	The final step is to guide your potential funders towards taking action. This could be in the form of investing in your journey, providing financial support, or even just expressing interest in learning more. Make it easy for them to take the next steps by providing clear instructions on how to get involved or make an investment.

How To Use It

The AIDA framework is crucial when seeking funding for your journey because it helps you structure your approach in a way that maximizes your chances of success:

- **Attracting funders**: In a competitive landscape, you need to capture the attention of potential investors or funders quickly. A well-crafted AIDA approach ensures you make a strong first impression.

- **Building Interest and Confidence**: It's not enough to just grab attention; you need to sustain it. By nurturing interest and desire, you help potential funders see the value and potential of your journey.

- **Converting Interest into Action**: Ultimately, your goal is to secure funding or support. The AIDA framework guides you in transitioning potential funders from a state of interest and desire to taking concrete actions that benefit your journey.

- **Effective Communication**: The framework also encourages clear and persuasive communication, ensuring that your message is compelling and easy to understand.

AIDA Applied

Here is an example of AIDA applied.

Attention: "Revolutionize Your Fitness Journey Today!"

- In this headline, we're grabbing the user's attention by using strong, action-oriented language and suggesting that our fitness app is a game-changer or they key to what you need. Notice how it says today, that is also a sense of urgency in the title that may grab someones attention.

Interest: "Discover Personalized Workouts and Nutrition Plans"

- Here, we're creating interest by highlighting the main features of the app, focusing on the personalized aspect, which is a unique selling point. We might add details about AI-driven recommendations and user success stories.

Desire: "Achieve Your Dream Body and Boost Your Confidence"

- Now, we're building desire by showing the benefits of using the app, such as achieving fitness goals and increasing self-confidence. Testimonials or before-and-after photos can enhance this section.

Action: "Download Now and Start Your Transformation!"

- Finally, we guide the user to take action by providing a clear call to action (CTA). In this case, it's to download the app and start using it immediately.

I hope by now you're seeing how all of these elements flow into each other. You need to have a well thought out idea, be able to have a framework to communicate it to clients, understand where your clients spend their time, who they are, and their desires to best have a business that is marketable to them. We havent even gotten to the heavy lifting yet, this is just the beginning of what you have to have in place to be attractive to people who are funding. Im proud of you for making it this far. Let's build out the AIDA for your products.

NOTE: I will add additional AIDA worksheets to the end of the workbook because I think that this should be done for each product you have and for each stage of the funnel (see the tie in?). You can use this as your marketing copy, or to answer certain grant questions that are targeted to your customer.

ACTIVITY

In this activity, you will apply the principles of the AIDA framework to your own product or project. By the end of this exercise, you will have a well-structured message that can help you pitch your idea to potential customers, investors, or stakeholders. This process will not only clarify your messaging but also increase your chances of success.

Remember, effective communication is key to achieving your goals, whether it's selling a product, securing funding, or garnering support for your project. The AIDA framework will help you create a message that engages your audience and drives them to take the desired action.

So, let's get started! Follow the steps outlined in this activity to outline the AIDA framework for your product or project, and by the end, you'll have a persuasive message that leaves a lasting impact on your target audience.

Product or Service:		Funnel Stage	

ATTENTION

The phrase that captures the users attention

INTEREST

What are your customers interest? How can you wrap that in a phrase?

DESIRE

What does yourcustomer desire? How can you communicate that you can meet their desires?

ACTION

What action do you want your customer to take based on their funnel stage?

Product or Service:		Funnel Stage	

ATTENTION

The phrase that captures the users attention

INTEREST

What are your customers interest? How can you wrap that in a phrase?

DESIRE

What does your customer desire? How can you communicate that you can meet their desires?

ACTION

What action do you want your customer to take based on their funnel stage?

Product or Service:		Funnel Stage	

ATTENTION

The phrase that captures the users attention

INTEREST

What are your customers interest? How can you wrap that in a phrase?

DESIRE

What does yourcustomer desire? How can you communicate that you can meet their desires?

ACTION

What action do you want your customer to take based on their funnel stage?

Product or Service:		Funnel Stage	

ATTENTION

The phrase that captures the users attention

INTEREST

What are your customers interest? How can you wrap that in a phrase?

DESIRE

What does your customer desire? How can you communicate that you can meet their desires?

ACTION

What action do you want your customer to take based on their funnel stage?

NOTES

NOTES

NOTES

Chapter 7

In this chapter we will wrap up the workbook and set us up to begin these concepts into action.

For our hands-on activity, we will set some goals, examine what we need to move forward, and plan for success.

Wrapping Up!

we're at the home stretch. Let's first talk about what you will need to make your project a success. The first activity will be looking at all of the items that you need to be successful. This can be software, inventory, advice, whatever it is, make a list. Then we will break down the cost. This will be IMPORTANT. Every grant application we have ever done ask us what you will do with the money, this start up cost breakdown will help you answer the question. Then we will outline a plan of success and chart how you know you're making progress. Last but not least we will set a goal we can hold you accountable to. Yup, this is were you take action. I don't want you to just read this book, I want you to put in the work and start putting your goals in action.

ACTIVITY ONE:
Outlining Required Items

The devil is in the details. Every intricate aspect, from design elements and materials to production processes and quality control, plays a pivotal role in shaping your product's success. It's akin to assembling a jigsaw puzzle, where each tiny piece represents a crucial element that contributes to the final picture.

These micro-details demand meticulous attention, as they directly impact the functionality, appeal, and overall value of your product. Whether you're crafting a physical item or a digital solution, the meticulous outlining of these micro-details is important. In this section, we will outline every peice of the puzzle that makes up your product.

Product Name:

Item Name	Justification

Product Name:

Item Name	Justification

Product Name:

Item Name	Justification

ACTIVITY TWO:
Outlining Start-Up Cost

Now that you've figured out what you need for your product and why, it's time to talk money! We're going to break down the costs for each part. This way, you'll know exactly how much cash you'll need to make your idea a reality. It's like making a shopping list for your project. Once we know the costs, you can plan your budget and figure out how to get the money you need to make it happen. So, let's get down to the details and figure out what it'll take to bring your product to life.

Start-Up Cost Product One	Cost	Annual	Monthly
Item			
Item			
Item			
Item			
Item			
Item			
Item			
Item			

NOTE: Some purchases are discounted when they are applied on an annual basis. Remember to ask and account for that price difference.

Start-Up Cost Product One	Cost	Annual	Monthly
Item			
Item			
Item			
Item			
Item			
Item			
Item			
Item			
Item			
Item			

Start-Up Cost Product One	Cost	Annual	Monthly
Item			
Item			
Item			
Item			
Item			
Item			
Item			
Item			
Item			
Item			
Item			

Fail To Plan, Plan To Fail

Now that we've got a handle on the costs, it's time to roll up our sleeves and plan for action! We'll use those cost breakdowns as our financial foundation for funding. But before we dive into securing the funds, we need a solid plan in place. That means figuring out what steps to take first, what resources we'll need to make it happen, and setting clear milestones to track our progress. It's like plotting the course for an exciting journey, and with this roadmap, we'll know exactly where we're headed and how to get there. So, let's get into the nitty-gritty of planning – what we'll do, what we'll need, and how we'll know when we've succeeded.

This is the last step. Once we've done this, this will help funders know that we have a well thought out plan for how we will be successful. This will let them know that you have thought about all the possible barriers and have created a plan to be successful. It's a way to demonstrate that you are not leaving anything to chance, but that you are an informed business owner that knows how to reach their audience and has a plan of success.

ACTIVITY THREE:
Goal Setting

Goal One

What Are 5 Steps I Need To Take?

Actions I Need To Take To Complete Each Step

Potential Problems & Potential Solutions

My Progress

Was I Successful?	Need More Work?	What Needs to Be Done?
☐ Yes	☐ Yes	
☐ No	☐ No	

Goal Two

What Are 5 Steps I Need To Take?

Actions I Need To Take To Complete Each Step

Potential Problems & Potential Solutions

My Progress

Was I Successful?	Need More Work?	What Needs to Be Done?
☐ Yes	☐ Yes	
☐ No	☐ No	

Goal Three

What Are 5 Steps I Need To Take?

Actions I Need To Take To Complete Each Step

Potential Problems & Potential Solutions

My Progress

Was I Successful?	Need More Work?	What Needs to Be Done?
☐ Yes	☐ Yes	
☐ No	☐ No	

NOTES

NOTES

NOTES

Chapter 8

OBJECTIVE

In this chapter we will explore the additional resources available through Mental Money to accelerate your journey to 6-figures in funding.

ACTIVITY

For our hands-on activity, you will sign up for the trainings, apply for, and access what you need right now to get funded.

That's it! You've made it! With this new found understanding, you are now ready to position yourself for funding. Unfortunatley it doesnt end here. This was just an entry level training to get you ready for the big leagues. The next leg is The Funding Formula. The Funding Formula training does even deeper into all of these elements and allows you to stand out from the competition with comprehensive assets (proposal, business plan, and pitch deck) and a system to automate the grant application process. If you are really looking to get into the six figure funding territory, that training is for you. We just open our application on a rolling basis to continuously accept new applicants into our program. Apply today!

THE FUNDING FORUMLA

A specialized training program meticulously crafted for black women in business. Our mission is to bridge the gap between dreams and tangible success by equipping you with the tools, knowledge, and resources essential to secure the funds you rightfully deserve.

COMMUNITY

the
Business
Bar

JOIN OUR GLOWING COMMUNITY THAT
COMES TOGETHER ONCE A MONTH TO
NETWORK AND GET FUNDING
INSIGHTS

Additional Resources

MENTAL MONEY PODCAST

A weekly podcast dedicated to providing you the tools you need to move forward in business.

SIX FIGURE GRANT WINNER COMMUNITY

This community is for the big leagues. For those who want to up-level their grant funding efforts in a community setting.

ADDITIONAL TRAININGS

STATE & LOCAL GOVERNMENT CONTRACTING

Learn what it takes to begin working with the government on the State & Local level. There are opportunites waiting for you!

BUSINESS CREDIT BASICS

start your business off on the right fiancial foot with business credit. Learn the high level strategy you need to keep your business credit worthy

COMING SOON

Join us as we become masters of our mind and money in 2024. Daily prompts and opportunites to uncover deep financial success.

"MOTIVATION IS LIKE A SHOWER,
YOU NEED IT DAILY"
-JIM ROHAN

SUBSCRIBE

Join us on Youtube where we have regularly updates on how you can be best supported along your business and funding journey.

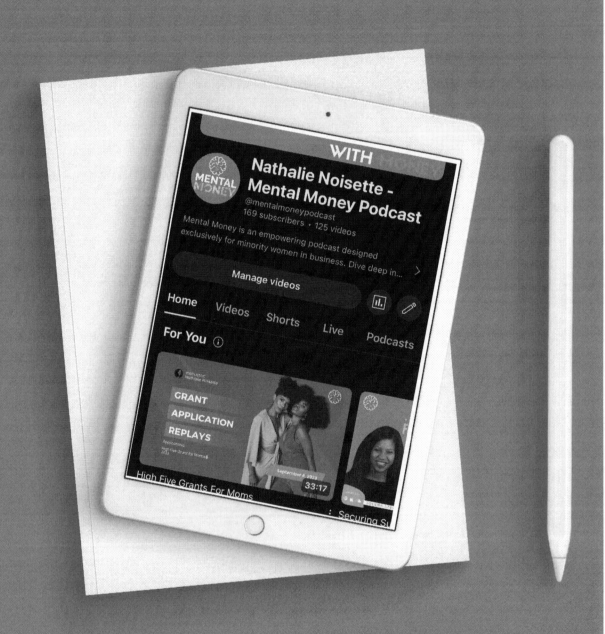

ADDITIONAL PAGES

Chapter 5: Product Outline Activity

Product or Service One:	
Customer motivation to buy the proposed solution.	

Top 3 similar products sold and their features

Top 3 similar products sold and the features their missing

What features could you offer that can add value?

Product or Service Two:	

Customer motivation to buy the proposed solution.

Top 3 similar products sold and their features

Top 3 similar products sold and the features their missing

What features could you offer that can add value?

Product or Service Three:	
Customer motivation to buy the proposed solution.	

Top 3 similar products sold and their features

Top 3 similar products sold and the features their missing

What features could you offer that can add value?

Product or Service Four:	
Customer motivation to buy the proposed solution.	

What features could you offer that can add value?

Top 3 similar products sold and the features their missing

What features could you offer that can add value?

CHAPTER 5: PRODUCT MATRIX ACTIVITY

Additional Products:

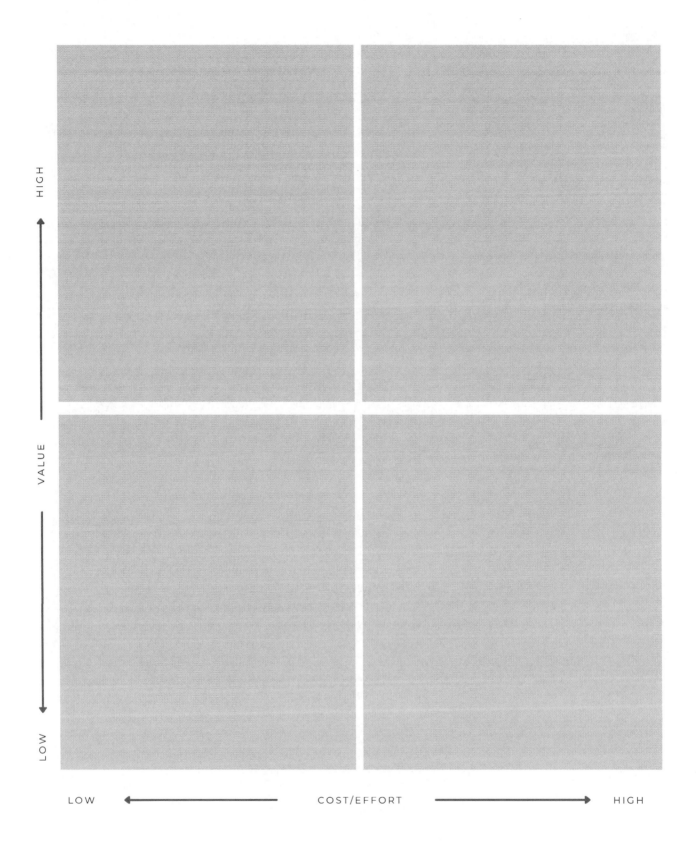

Additional Products:

Additional Products:

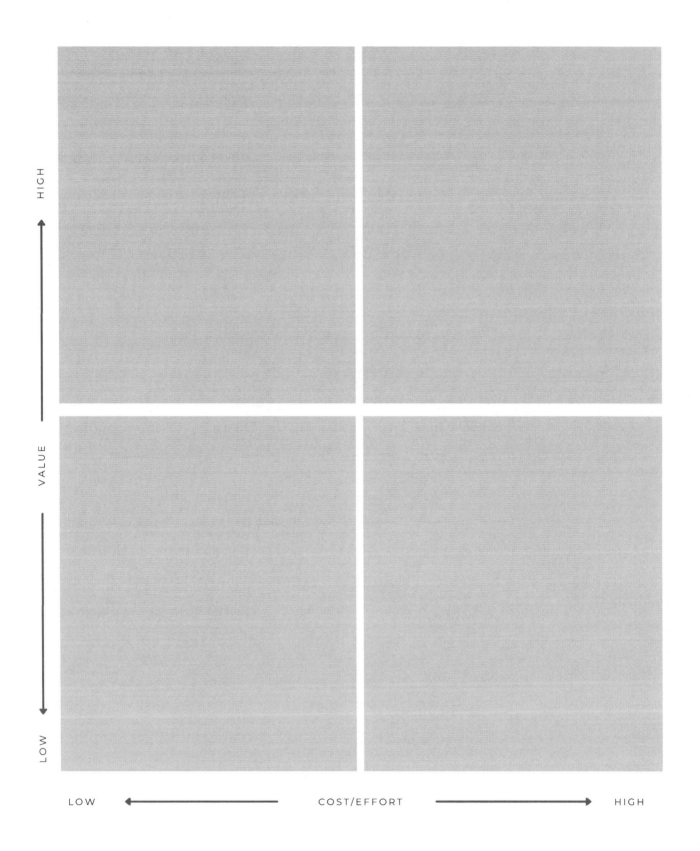

HIGH

VALUE

LOW

LOW ← COST/EFFORT → HIGH

Additional Products:

HIGH

VALUE

LOW

LOW — COST/EFFORT — HIGH

Additional Products:

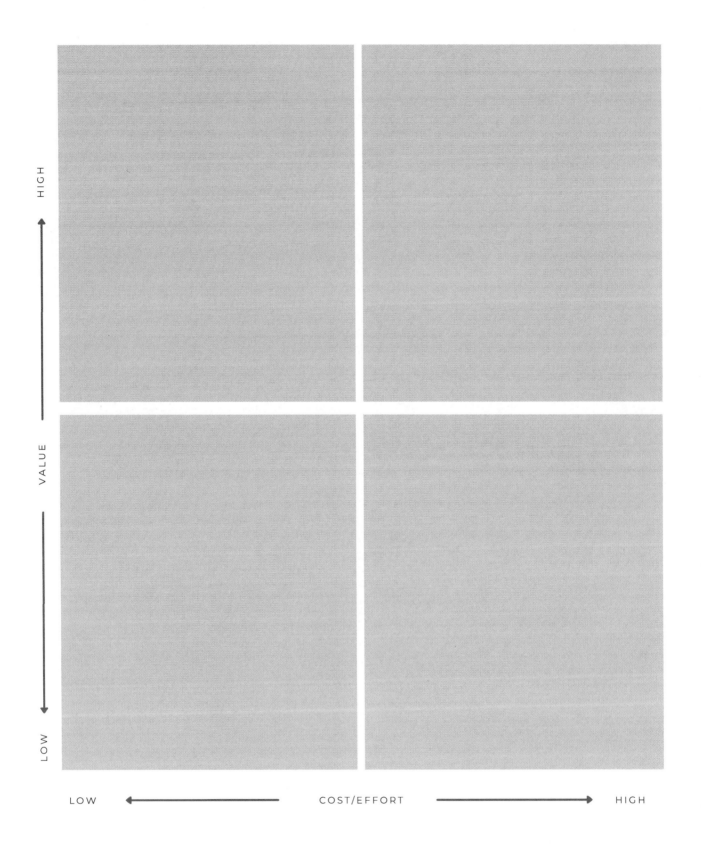

Chapter 5: Competitor Analysis

Secondary Competition (aka Indirect Competitor)

What problems do they solve?

What is your competition really good at?

Where is there room for improvement?

What do they do to reach their target audience?

Where do they go to reach their target audience?

How are they pricing their products?

Additional Competition

What problems do they solve?

What is your competition really good at?

Where is there room for improvement?

What do they do to reach their target audience?

Where do they go to reach their target audience?

How are they pricing their products?

Chapter 6:
AIDA Activity

Product or Service:		Funnel Stage	

ATTENTION

The phrase that captures the users attention

INTEREST

What are your customers interest? How can you wrap that in a phrase?

DESIRE

What does yourcustomer desire? How can you communicate that you can meet their desires?

ACTION

What action do you want your customer to take based on their funnel stage?

Product or Service:		Funnel Stage	

ATTENTION

The phrase that captures the users attention

INTEREST

What are your customers interest? How can you wrap that in a phrase?

DESIRE

What does your customer desire? How can you communicate that you can meet their desires?

ACTION

What action do you want your customer to take based on their funnel stage?

Product or Service:		Funnel Stage	

ATTENTION

The phrase that captures the users attention

INTEREST

What are your customers interest? How can you wrap that in a phrase?

DESIRE

What does yourcustomer desire? How can you communicate that you can meet their desires?

ACTION

What action do you want your customer to take based on their funnel stage?

Product or Service:		Funnel Stage	

ATTENTION

The phrase that captures the users attention

INTEREST

What are your customers interest? How can you wrap that in a phrase?

DESIRE

What does yourcustomer desire? How can you communicate that you can meet their desires?

ACTION

What action do you want your customer to take based on their funnel stage?

Product or Service:		Funnel Stage	

ATTENTION

The phrase that captures the users attention

INTEREST

What are your customers interest? How can you wrap that in a phrase?

DESIRE

What does your customer desire? How can you communicate that you can meet their desires?

ACTION

What action do you want your customer to take based on their funnel stage?

Product or Service:		Funnel Stage	

ATTENTION

The phrase that captures the users attention

INTEREST

What are your customers interest? How can you wrap that in a phrase?

DESIRE

What does yourcustomer desire? How can you communicate that you can meet their desires?

ACTION

What action do you want your customer to take based on their funnel stage?

Product or Service:		Funnel Stage	

ATTENTION

The phrase that captures the users attention

INTEREST

What are your customers interest? How can you wrap that in a phrase?

DESIRE

What does yourcustomer desire? How can you communicate that you can meet their desires?

ACTION

What action do you want your customer to take based on their funnel stage?

Product or Service:		Funnel Stage	

ATTENTION

The phrase that captures the users attention

INTEREST

What are your customers interest? How can you wrap that in a phrase?

DESIRE

What does yourcustomer desire? How can you communicate that you can meet their desires?

ACTION

What action do you want your customer to take based on their funnel stage?

Product or Service:		Funnel Stage	

ATTENTION

The phrase that captures the users attention

INTEREST

What are your customers interest? How can you wrap that in a phrase?

DESIRE

What does your customer desire? How can you communicate that you can meet their desires?

ACTION

What action do you want your customer to take based on their funnel stage?

Product or Service:		Funnel Stage	

ATTENTION

The phrase that captures the users attention

INTEREST

What are your customers interest? How can you wrap that in a phrase?

DESIRE

What does yourcustomer desire? How can you communicate that you can meet their desires?

ACTION

What action do you want your customer to take based on their funnel stage?

Product or Service:		Funnel Stage	

ATTENTION

The phrase that captures the users attention

INTEREST

What are your customers interest? How can you wrap that in a phrase?

DESIRE

What does yourcustomer desire? How can you communicate that you can meet their desires?

ACTION

What action do you want your customer to take based on their funnel stage?

Product or Service:		Funnel Stage	

ATTENTION

The phrase that captures the users attention

INTEREST

What are your customers interest? How can you wrap that in a phrase?

DESIRE

What does yourcustomer desire? How can you communicate that you can meet their desires?

ACTION

What action do you want your customer to take based on their funnel stage?

Product or Service:		Funnel Stage	

ATTENTION

The phrase that captures the users attention

INTEREST

What are your customers interest? How can you wrap that in a phrase?

DESIRE

What does yourcustomer desire? How can you communicate that you can meet their desires?

ACTION

What action do you want your customer to take based on their funnel stage?

Product or Service:		Funnel Stage	

ATTENTION

The phrase that captures the users attention

INTEREST

What are your customers interest? How can you wrap that in a phrase?

DESIRE

What does yourcustomer desire? How can you communicate that you can meet their desires?

ACTION

What action do you want your customer to take based on their funnel stage?

Product or Service:		Funnel Stage	

ATTENTION

The phrase that captures the users attention

INTEREST

What are your customers interest? How can you wrap that in a phrase?

DESIRE

What does yourcustomer desire? How can you communicate that you can meet their desires?

ACTION

What action do you want your customer to take based on their funnel stage?

NOTES

NOTES

NOTES

NOTES

NOTES

NOTES

NOTES

NOTES

NOTES

NOTES

NOTES

NOTES

NOTES

NOTES

NOTES

NOTES

NOTES

NOTES

NOTES

NOTES

NOTES

NOTES

NOTES

NOTES

NOTES

NOTES

NOTES

NOTES

NOTES

NOTES

NOTES

NOTES

NOTES

NOTES

NOTES

NOTES

NOTES

NOTES

NOTES

NOTES

NOTES

NOTES

Made in the USA
Columbia, SC
22 April 2024

34739828R00139